# GETAWAY
## *Home*

*your stories and adventures from your
home away from home*

— A GUIDED JOURNAL —

Strolls, Parks, Shops

Dinner Decisions

Gone Fishing

*Michelle Serafini*

Whether you leave this journal in your getaway home or

take it with you to the places you stay

that you consider your getaway home, may you use this

journal to help remember experiences, share your memories,

and document all the moments, big and small, that make

your home away from home special.

*Michelle Serafini*

## SHARE STORIES

The summer home, the beach cottage, the lake cabin, the pied-à-terre,

the ski chalet or the ocean retreat, no matter what you call your

getaway home, this is the place where you

recharge, rejuvenate, and reconnect.

Sometimes you spend a weekend, sometimes all summer,

sometimes the holidays, and sometimes you share

your getaway home with others.

Sometimes your getaway home isn't a house, it's an RV,

a tent, a yurt, or a boat. Whether you own

or rent your getaway home, your experiences there

expand your mind, help you reset and

forever change the lens through which you see the world.

Let this journal allow you to be a storyteller of adventures,

a food critic of local restaurants, a travel writer and guide.

And may your adventures, big and small,

create lifelong stories to be shared.

"Travel leaves you speechless,
then it turns you into a storyteller."
Ibn Battu

My getaway home means so much to me because...        /        /

_____

_____

_____

_____

_____

_____

_____

_____

There is nothing like stepping out of the plane
and feeling the thick air of the tropics hug
your body, the ocean breeze caressing your face,
because in that moment your
tropical getaway begins.

*palm trees*

*coconuts*

*tanned skin*

*sunsets*

*warm nights*

*starry skies*

*salt*

Today I saw...                                                    /      /

_____

_____

_____

_____

_____

_____

_____

_____

Looking around I saw...                                                    /        /

Today's best experience was...                                             /        /

*At our getaway home,
we wander the neighborhoods,
visit markets, sit in cafes,
stroll through parks, and
chat with shopkeepers.*

Today I ate...                                                    /      /

_____
_____
_____
_____
_____
_____

The food and drinks I liked the most were...                      /      /

_____
_____
_____
_____
_____
_____

"Water is the driving force of
all nature."
Leonardo da Vinci

As the sun rose...                    /        /

_____
_____
_____
_____
_____
_____
_____
_____
_____

As the sun set...                     /        /

_____
_____
_____
_____
_____
_____
_____
_____
_____
_____
_____

Outing checklist...                    /        /

_____
_____
_____
_____
_____
_____
_____
_____

Favorite activities...                 /        /

_____
_____
_____
_____
_____
_____
_____
_____

Today I hung out with...                                    /        /

_____

_____

_____

_____

These moments brought me serenity...                        /        /

_____

_____

_____

_____

The desert is like a powerful magnet.
It changes those who come within its field.
No matter the location,
the vast expanses, the colors, and the serenity
are magical and inspiring.

Our favorite activities are...                                              /        /

_____

_____

_____

_____

*When we are here, we say yes to adventures, game nights, picnics, bonfires, hammocks, and kitchen dancing.*

The best places to take walks are...                                        /        /

_____

_____

_____

_____

We rest and rejuvenate by...                                                    /          /

_____

_____

_____

_____

_____

*Our getaway home helps relieve stress and boredom, provides a change of scenery, and brings perspective to our daily lives.*

The best scenery is...                                                          /          /

_____

_____

_____

_____

_____

run

piste

powder

schuss

slalom

skis

snowboard

snow

après-ski

Being at my home away from home creates experiences that allow          /          /
me not to try to escape life but rather for life not to escape me...

It was at that moment...                                    /          /

_____

_____

_____

_____

_____

_____

_____

_____

_____

*We live each day
as locals.*

The sights and the sounds...                                    /        /

_____
_____
_____
_____
_____
_____

The people who inspire...                                       /        /

_____
_____
_____
_____
_____
_____
_____

When we are here with family or friends we...          /          /

_____
_____
_____
_____
_____
_____
_____
_____

At the beach we...          /          /

_____
_____
_____
_____
_____
_____
_____
_____

*In the end, kids won't remember that fancy toy or game.*
*They will remember the times we have spent together.*

At the lake we....          /          /

_____
_____
_____
_____
_____
_____
_____
_____

At the river we...          /          /

_____
_____
_____
_____
_____
_____
_____
_____

"Twenty years from now you will be more
disappointed by the things you didn't do
than by the ones you did.
So, throw off the bowlines.
Sail away from the safe harbor.
Catch the trade winds in your sails.
Explore. Dream. Discover."
Mark Twain

*"All any of us need is a very light suitcase."*
*Oswald Wynd*

My preferred suitcase is...

☐ soft-sided suitcase

☐ hard-sided suitcase

☐ backpack

☐ rolling backpack

☐ duffel bag

☐ tote bag

☐ _____

☐ _____

☐ _____

☐ _____

My preferred mode of travel is...

- ☐ plane
- ☐ train
- ☐ SUV
- ☐ RV
- ☐ convertible
- ☐ boat
- ☐ _____
- ☐ _____
- ☐ _____
- ☐ _____

The most unusual mode of transportation
I have taken is...

- ☐ tuk tuk
- ☐ pedicab
- ☐ tandem bike
- ☐ vaporetto
- ☐ funicular
- ☐ scooter
- ☐ _____
- ☐ _____
- ☐ _____
- ☐ _____

"Take only memories.
Leave only footprints."
Chief Seattle, Suquamish Chief

In the quiet of the morning....          /          /

_____
_____
_____
_____
_____
_____
_____

At high noon...          /          /

_____
_____
_____
_____
_____
_____
_____

*To connect to nature is to connect to yourself.*
*There are hidden pockets of beauty all around.*

At dusk...          /          /

_____
_____
_____
_____
_____
_____
_____

About last night...          /          /

_____
_____
_____
_____
_____
_____
_____

Our favorite picnic spots are...                                                      /        /

_____

_____

_____

_____

_____

Our favorite farmers markets are...                                                   /        /

_____

_____

_____

_____

_____

Favorite ethnic food...

1 _____

2 _____

3 _____

4 _____

5 _____

Favorite food to grill...

1 _____

2 _____

3 _____

4 _____

5 _____

Favorite ice cream and gelato...

1 _____

2 _____

3 _____

4 _____

5 _____

Favorite dessert place...

1 _____

2 _____

3 _____

4 _____

5 _____

A river runs through it...                                    /        /

_____

_____

_____

_____

_____

_____

_____

_____

Wildlife we have seen or heard...                            /        /

_____

_____

_____

_____

_____

_____

_____

_____

_____

_____

"I grew up with the smell of the
lake and the feeling of the woods."
Steven Tyler

Random thoughts...          /          /

One way to tackle a bad mood
is to enjoy a day on a dock
and jump into a lake!

When I've taken everything in, I close my eyes for a moment like a camera shutter
and then see in my mind...                                    /        /

It was at that moment...                                    /        /

_____

_____

_____

_____

_____

_____

_____

_____

lobster & clam bakes

corn on the cob

coleslaw & potato salad

cobbler & ice cream

cheers

At the summer house, time slows,
stories become legends, and
the bond of love grows.

Spring beginnings...                                    /        /

_____
_____
_____
_____
_____

Summer loves...                                         /        /

_____
_____
_____
_____
_____

Autumn hues...                                              /        /

_____

_____

_____

_____

_____

Winter scenes...                                            /        /

_____

_____

_____

_____

_____

Last night on the porch...                                    /          /

_____

_____

_____

_____

_____

_____

_____

_____

My favorite place to sit around a bonfire is ...

☐ a beach in Mexico

☐ a campfire in the Grand Canyon

☐ the Boundary Waters

☐ a lake retreat

☐ a yoga retreat in the desert

☐ at our cabin

☐ _____

☐ _____

☐ _____

☐ _____

My favorite outdoor chairs are...

☐ adirondack

☐ hammock

☐ lawn chair

☐ pool chaise loungers

☐ beach chairs

☐ patio swings

☐ _____

☐ _____

☐ _____

☐ _____

I am a child of the ocean
and the land is my second home.

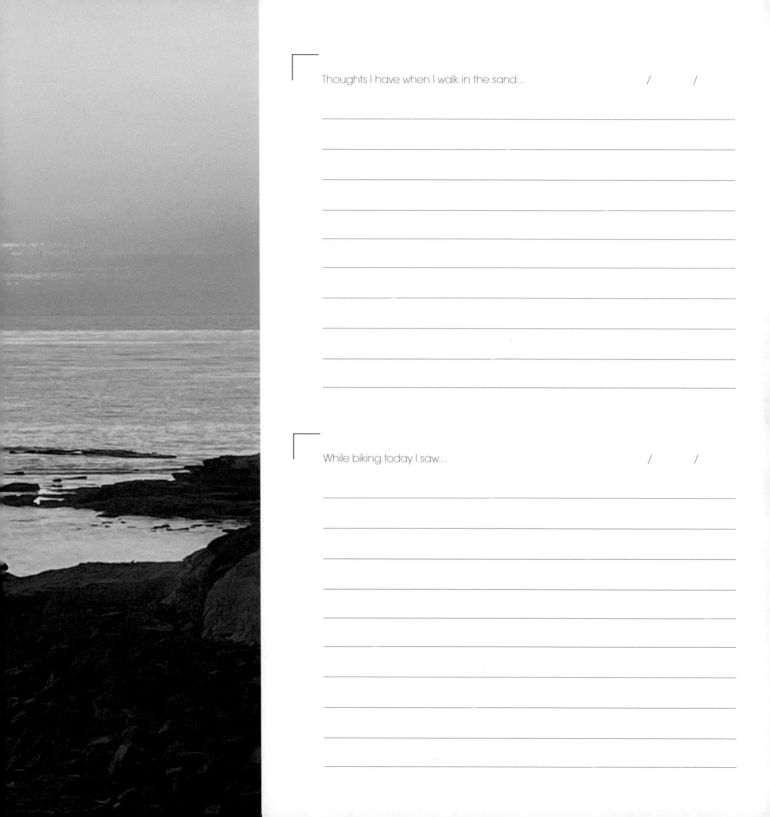

Thoughts I have when I walk in the sand...                    /        /

_____

_____

_____

_____

_____

_____

_____

_____

_____

While biking today I saw...                              /        /

_____

_____

_____

_____

_____

_____

_____

_____

_____

_____

It was at that moment...                                    /        /

Today we drew our own lines
on the canvas of fresh powder snow.

Right here...                                                                    /        /

_____

_____

_____

_____

_____

_____

_____

_____

Right now...                                                      /        /

Best food joints...

1 _____

2 _____

3 _____

4 _____

5 _____

Best food memories...

1 _____

2 _____

3 _____

4 _____

5 _____

Best happy hours...

1 _____

2 _____

3 _____

4 _____

5 _____

Best pubs and breweries...

1 _____

2 _____

3 _____

4 _____

5 _____

Best coffee shops...

1 _____

2 _____

3 _____

4 _____

5 _____

Best restaurants...

1 _____

2 _____

3 _____

4 _____

5 _____

Best sandwich shops...

1 _____

2 _____

3 _____

4 _____

5 _____

Best kitchen and wine bars...

1 _____

2 _____

3 _____

4 _____

5 _____

*Summer is when laziness*
*finds respectability.*

Musings...                                                    /        /

_____
_____
_____
_____
_____
_____
_____
_____
_____
_____
_____
_____
_____
_____
_____
_____
_____
_____
_____
_____
_____

Our favorite pastimes at our getaway home are...                    /          /

_____

_____

_____

_____

_____

_____

_____

_____

_____

_____

_____

_____

_____

_____

_____

_____

_____

_____

_____

_____

The warm breeze, the scent of freshly cut grass,
the stunning vistas, and the serenity that
surrounds me as I make my approach.

Say yes to adventure…

My getaway home footwear includes...

☐ flip-flops

☐ snow boots

☐ hiking boots

☐ running shoes

☐ sandals

☐ trekking shoes

☐ water shoes

☐ waders

☐ rain boots

☐ clogs

☐ boat shoes

☐ riding boots

☐ cowboy boots

☐ heels

☐ wedges

☐ loafers

☐ _____

☐ _____

☐ _____

☐ _____

My getaway home outerwear includes...

- ☐ cotton sweater
- ☐ rain jacket
- ☐ fleece jacket
- ☐ ski jacket
- ☐ wool coat
- ☐ pashmina
- ☐ sweatshirt
- ☐ hoodie
- ☐ leather jacket
- ☐ wool sweater
- ☐ jean jacket
- ☐ down coat
- ☐ peacoat
- ☐ trench coat
- ☐ biker jacket
- ☐ bomber jacket
- ☐ _____
- ☐ _____
- ☐ _____
- ☐ _____

At my getaway home I...

- ☐ watch TV
- ☐ don't watch TV
- ☐ watch movies
- ☐ read novels
- ☐ flip through magazines
- ☐ play board games
- ☐ play cards
- ☐ listen to music
- ☐ listen to podcasts
- ☐ listen to birds
- ☐ listen to nature's sounds
- ☐ grill my favorite foods
- ☐ write and journal
- ☐ take naps
- ☐ get up with the sun
- ☐ sleep in
- ☐ _____
- ☐ _____
- ☐ _____
- ☐ _____

When it's quiet...                                                    /      /

The best things in life are the people
we love, the places we've been, and the memories
we've made along the way.

As the waves roll in...                    /        /

The places I consider my home away from home...          /          /

_____

_____

_____

_____

_____

_____

_____

_____

_____

_____

_____

_____

_____

_____

_____

_____

_____

_____

_____

_____

_____

Not all
who
wander
are lost.

The flora and fauna I see...                                    /        /

_____

_____

_____

_____

_____

The waterways are...                                           /        /

_____

_____

_____

_____

_____

The scenery is breathtaking because...                                    /        /

_____

_____

_____

_____

_____

The colors that surround me are...                                        /        /

_____

_____

_____

_____

_____

What saying yes to adventure means to me...                    /        /

"The sea, once it
casts its spell,
holds one in its net
of wonder forever."
Jacques Cousteau

I woke to...          /     /

_____
_____
_____
_____
_____
_____
_____

I fell asleep to...          /     /

_____
_____
_____
_____
_____
_____
_____
_____

I listened to...        /      /

_____

_____

_____

_____

_____

_____

_____

_____

I read...        /      /

_____

_____

_____

_____

_____

_____

_____

_____

I am grateful for...                                        /      /

_____

_____

_____

_____

_____

_____

*When something good happens,*
*we go to our getaway home to celebrate.*
*When something bad happens, we go to forget.*
*If nothing is happening, we go to make something happen!*

_____

_____

_____

_____

_____

_____

_____

The ways travel has changed me...                                    /      /

_____

_____

_____

_____

_____

_____

_____

_____

*" A mind that is stretched by a new experience*
*can never go back to its old dimensions."*
*Oliver Wendell Holmes*

_____

_____

_____

_____

_____

_____

_____

_____

_____

I feel most alive when...                                    /        /

_____

_____

_____

_____

_____

_____

_____

_____

_____

_____

_____

_____

_____

_____

_____

_____

_____

_____

Never get so busy
making a living, you forget to
make a life.

My perfect day includes...                                    /        /

_____

_____

_____

_____

_____

_____

_____

_____

_____

_____

_____

_____

_____

_____

_____

_____

_____

_____

_____

_____

_____

_____

_____

The things I like most about my home away from home...          /          /

_____
_____
_____
_____
_____
_____
_____
_____
_____
_____
_____

The people who inspire me most are...                                    /        /

_____

_____

_____

_____

_____

_____

The things that inspire me most are...                                   /        /

_____

_____

_____

_____

_____

_____

_____

My fondest memory is...                                    /        /

_____
_____
_____
_____
_____

My future hope is...                                        /        /

_____
_____
_____
_____
_____

The most peaceful place I've been is...                                    /        /

_____

_____

_____

_____

_____

The most fascinating place I've been is...                                  /        /

_____

_____

_____

_____

_____

Towering trees line the edge of the rocky
coastline drench in mist and fog, creating a scene
that resembles an impressionist painting.

I find wonder and awe in...                                    /        /

_____

_____

_____

_____

_____

_____

_____

_____

_____

As I take a deep breath I notice...                           /        /

_____

_____

_____

_____

_____

_____

_____

_____

_____

_____

Our favorite outdoor places are...                                    /         /

_____

_____

_____

_____

_____

_____

_____

_____

_____

Our favorite indoor places are...                                    /         /

_____

_____

_____

_____

_____

_____

_____

_____

_____

Bucket list...                                                    /      /

_____
_____
_____
_____
_____
_____
_____
_____
_____
_____
_____
_____
_____
_____
_____
_____
_____
_____

Bucket list...                                                          /        /

_____

_____

_____

_____

_____

_____

_____

_____

_____

_____

_____

_____

_____

_____

_____

_____

_____

_____

Michelle Serafini is a travel and lifestyle writer, speaker and coastal Realtor

based in La Jolla, California. Her love for travel and staying in getaway homes

around the globe inspired her to create this guided journal.

To find out more about her travel adventures and lifestyle tips,

visit ANoteFromTheCoast.com or follow her @anotefromthecoast.

# PHOTO LOCATIONS + PHOTOGRAPHERS

Cover | Wailea Beach, Maui, Hawaii | Michelle Serafini
Inside Title Page 1 | London, England; Granville Island Market, Vancouver BC, Canada; San Diego, CA | Michelle Serafini
Pages 2-3 | Pacific Beach, CA | Michelle Serafini
Pages 4-5 | Puerto Vallarta, Mexico | Michelle Serafini
Pages 6-7 | Naples, FL; Maui, HI | Michelle Serafini
Pages 8-9 | Rome, IT; Christmas Market, Bolzano, IT; Borough Market, London; Granville Island Market, Vancouver BC; Neighborhood Market, Paris, FR | Michelle Serafini
Pages 10-11 | Glass Beach, Fort Bragg, CA | Franco Serafini
Pages 12-13 | Tribu, Todos Santos & Tribu, Pescadero, Baja California Sur, MX; Serpent Sculpture, Borrego Springs, CA | Michelle Serafini
Pages 14-15 | South Rim, Grand Canyon National Park, Arizona | Franco Serafini
Pages 16-17 | Jackson Hole, Wyoming | Shanon Jensen
Pages 18-19 | Mendocino, CA; Tynemouth, North Shields, UK; Rancho Santa Fe, CA; Santa Fe, NM; Conyers, GA | Katherine Rupp & Michelle Serafini
Page 21 | Scripps Pier, La Jolla, CA | Michelle Serafini
Pages 22-23 | Mirror Lake, Fiordland National Park, South Island, New Zealand | Franco Serafini
Page 24 | Big Tesuque, Santa Fe National Forest, NM | Franco Serafini
Page 26 | Mendocino, CA; Queenstown Gardens, Queenstown, New Zealand | Franco Serafini
Page 27 | Santa Fe, NM; Burger Joint, NYC, NY; Fürst, Cafe-Konditorei, Salzburg, Austria; Fauna, Valle de Guadalupe, Baja, MX; Funkenhausen, Chicago, IL.; Beer Church, New Buffalo, MI | Katherine Rupp & Michelle Serafini
Pages 28-29 | Fiordland National Park, South Island, New Zealand | Franco Serafini
Page 30 | London, England | Michelle Serafini
Page 31 | Bleggio, Trento, Italy; Newcastle upon Tyne, England; Amsterdam, Netherlands | Michelle Serafini & Katherine Rupp
Page 32 | Lake in Northern Wisconsin | Renee Palmer
Page 34 | San Diego Bay, San Diego, CA | Michelle Serafini
Page 35 | Lake Michigan, MI | Jonathan Rupp
Pages 36-37 | Loreto Bay, Nopoló, Loreto Baja Peninsula, Mexico | Michelle Serafini
Page 38 | River Belle Inn, Healdsburg, CA | Franco Serafini
Page 39 | Hotel del Coronado, Coronado, CA | Michelle Serafini
Pages 40-41 | Bird Rock, La Jolla, CA | Michelle Serafini
Pages 42-43 | Breckenridge, CO | Shanon Jensen
Pages 44-45 | Tribu, Todos Santos, B.C.S., MX | Michelle Serafini
Page 46 | Rustic Ridge Vineyards, Jamul, CA; Hualtuco, Oaxaca, MX; Birreria Pedavena, Trento, IT; Regency Cafe, London, England | Michelle Serafini & Katherine Rupp
Page 47 | Strudel, Innsbruck, AT; Fergbaker, Queenstown, NZ; Cafe Sacher, Vienna AT; Noble Folk Ice Cream & Pie Bar, Healdsburg, CA | Michelle Serafini & Franco Serafini
Pages 48-49 | Pacific Beach, CA | Michelle Serafini
Pages 50-51 | Torrey Pines Golf Course, San Diego, CA | Michelle Serafini
Pages 52-53 | Mismaloya Beach, Mismaloya, Jalisco, Mexico | Michelle Serafini
Page 55 | Waterfall, Piopiotahi (Milford Sound) Marine Reserve, New Zealand | Michelle Serafini
Pages 56-57 | Playas Rosarito, Rosarito, B.C., Mexico | Franco Serafini
Page 59 | Tribu, Pescadero, B.C.S., Mexico | Michelle Serafini
Page 60-61 | Heritage House Resort and Spa, Mendocino Coast, California | Michelle Serafini
Page 63 | Danzante Bay, Loreto, Baja Peninsula, MX | Franco Serafini
Pages 64-65 | Encinitas, CA | Michelle Serafini
Pages 66-67 | Sea of Cortez, San Felipe, Mexico | Franco Serafini
Page 68 | Anaheim, CA | Michelle Serafini
Page 71 | California Coast | Franco Serafini
Page 72-73 | La Jolla Cove, La Jolla, CA | Michelle Serafini
Page 74 | Los Cabos, MX; Lake Michigan, Chicago, IL; Redwood Forest, Northern CA | Michelle Serafini & Katherine Rupp
Page 75 | Hyde Park, London, UK; Sawyer Home & Garden Center, Sawyer, MI; Union Pier, MI | Michelle Serafini
Pages 76-77 | Breckenridge Ski Resort, Colorado | Shanon Jensen
Pages 78-79 | Heritage House Resort in Little River on the Mendocino Coast, CA | Franco Serafini
Page 81 | Vancouver, British Columbia, Canada | Franco Serafini
Pages 82-83 | Koi Pond, Kohala Coast, Big Island, Hawaii | Michelle Serafini
Pages 84-85 | Wailea Beach, Maui, Hawaii | Michelle Serafini
Page 85 | Author Picture | Jenna Selby
Back Cover | Maui, HI; Ski Lift, Matterhorn, Switzerland | Encuentro Guadalupe, Valle de Guadalupe, Baja, MX | Mijas, Costa Del Sol, Spain | Shanon Jensen & Michelle Serafini

Archway Publishing books may be ordered through booksellers or by contacting:

Archway Publishing
1663 Liberty Drive
Bloomington, IN 47403
www.archwaypublishing.com
844-669-3957

Because of the dynamic nature of the Internet, any web addresses or links contained in this book may have changed since publication and may no longer be valid. The views expressed in this work are solely those of the author and do not necessarily reflect the views of the publisher, and the publisher hereby disclaims any responsibility for them.

Photography by Michelle Serafini, Franco Serafini, Katherine Rupp, Jonathan Rupp, Shanon Leder Jensen, Renee Palmer and Jenna Selby.
Book design by Renee Palmer

ISBN: 978-1-6657-2878-2 (sc)
ISBN: 978-1-6657-2880-5 (hc)
ISBN: 978-1-6657-2879-9 (e)

Print information available on the last page.

Archway Publishing rev. date: 08/24/2023

Printed in the United States
by Baker & Taylor Publisher Services